# SHEFFIELD'S REMARKABLE

*Presented by*
ROGER REDFERN

The Cottage Press,
Old Brampton, Chesterfield, Derbyshire

# CONTENTS

| | | | |
|---|---|---|---|
| Introduction | 4 | Oak House | 27 |
| Manor Lodge | 5 | Stumperlowe Cottage | 28, 29 |
| Queen's Tower | 6 | Stumperlowe Hall | 30, 31 |
| Shrewsbury Hospital | 7 | Fulwood Hall | 32 |
| Old Queen's Head | 8 | Whiteley Wood Hall | 33 |
| Leader House | 9 | Dore Moor House | 34 |
| Old Bank House | 10 | Beauchief Hall | 35 |
| Paradise Square | 11 | Whirlow Brook House | 36 |
| The Mount | 12 | Whirlow Hall | 37 |
| Broom Hall | 13 | Whirlow House | 38 |
| 23, Corporation Street | 14 | Whirlow Court | 39 |
| Carbrook Hall | 15 | Parkhead Hall | 40 |
| Birley Old Hall | 16 | Mylnhurst | 41 |
| Wadsley Hall | 17 | Banner Cross Hall | 42, 43 |
| Loxley House | 18 | Shirle Hill | 43 |
| The Towers | 19 | Kenwood | 44, 45 |
| Tapton Hall | 20 | 6, Kenwood Road | 45 |
| Thornbury | 21 | Mount Pleasant | 46 |
| Endcliffe Hall | 22, 23 | Bishops' House | 47 |
| Oakbrook | 24, 25 | The Oakes in Norton | 48 |
| Riverdale House | 26 | Beech Mill | back cover |

## ACKNOWLEDGMENTS

My thanks go to those several proprietors who gave permission to photograph their properties and to John Baker, J. D. Campbell. Eddie Gorman, Sir Eric Mensforth, Daniel Peck, Sir Reresby Sitwell and the Yorkshire and Humberside TAVR Association for their invaluable help.

Copyright Roger Redfern 1996

ISBN 0 9519148 3 9

British Library Cataloguing in Publication Data

Printed by B. R. Hubbard (Printers) Ltd., Dronfield, 1996

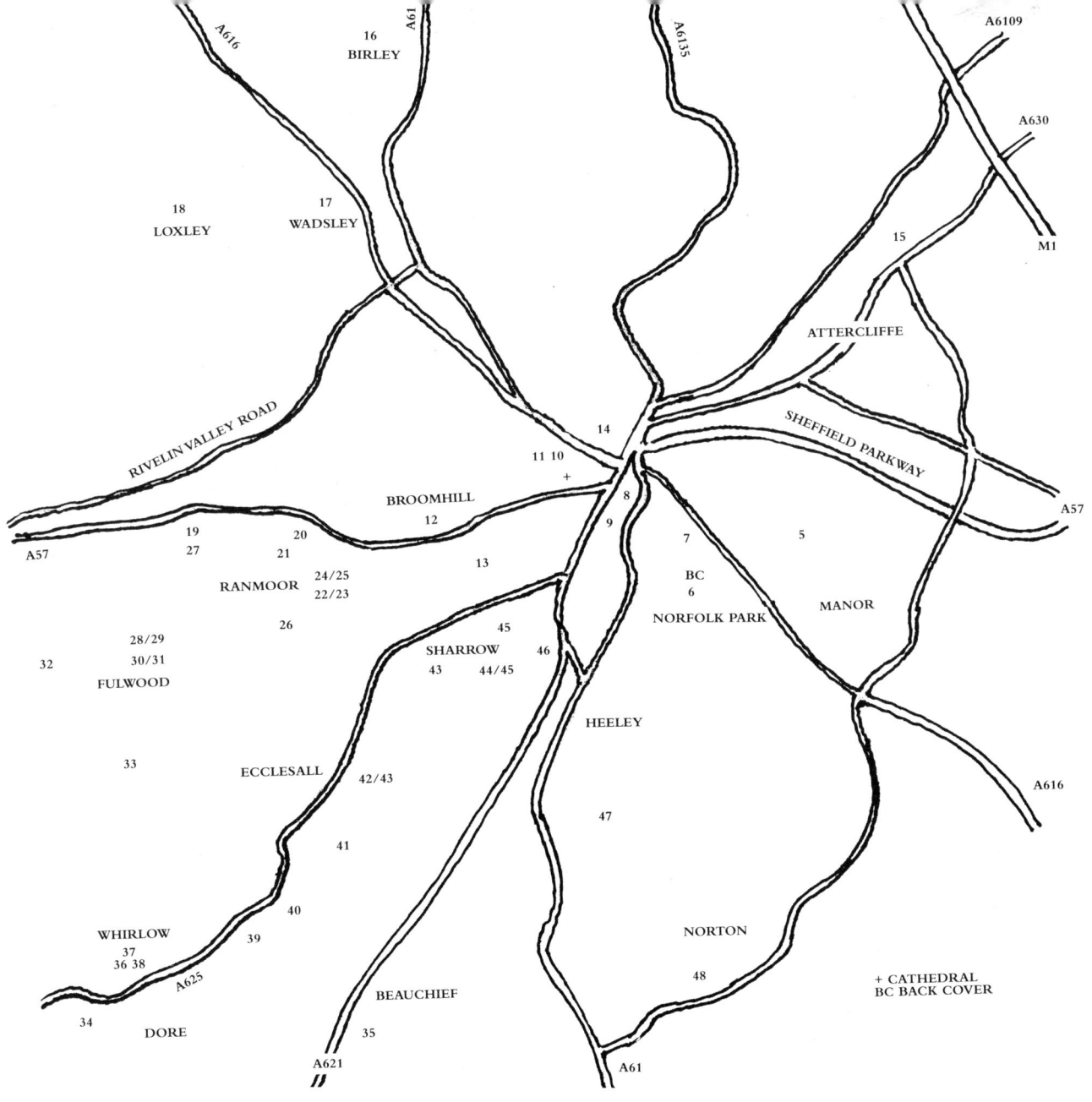

*Numbers on the map refer to pages (see opposite).*

# Sheffield's Remarkable Houses

Sir Nikolaus Pevsner did not mince his words, he considered the architecture of Sheffield "a miserable disappointment." Certainly the city has few really old buildings of any merit – the Cathedral, the ruins of Manor Lodge and a trio of timber-framed houses is about the extent of it. This is rather a surprise when we remember that it had assumed importance as a centre for cutlery and edge tool manufacture by the sixteenth century. It can't be assumed that most of the early architectural gems have been swept away, alongside the modest buildings of the medieval maze near the old heart of the town. However, innovations in steel making came a hundred years later than those in, say, textile manufacturing so many old buildings must have been lost in the fifty years of fast growth between 1870 and 1920, buildings of a type which survived in other towns where the pace of development was slower at that particular time.

What mustn't be forgotten is that a considerable remnant of eighteenth century development remains tucked away on three sides of the Cathedral – gems that include the former Girls' Charity School (1786), former Boys' Charity School (1825), Old Bank House (1728) and, of course, the pre-eminent Georgian ensemble of Paradise Square (1736, 1771).

The houses described here are, naturally, a personal choice; certainly by no means an exhaustive coverage of Sheffield's remarkable houses. With one exception all those included still exist (only Whiteley Wood Hall has gone, though its stable block still stands) and most are listed Grade 11 or above. There are houses from the nationally important (like Manor Lodge) ranging through early timber-framed (like Broom Hall), seventeenth century yeomen's farmhouses (Fulwood Hall), eighteenth century town houses (Mount Pleasant), impressive nineteenth century houses of the new rich (Oakbrook and Endcliffe Hall), and a late twentieth century superhome (Whirlow House).

Most have at least some architectural merit though some have really been included for their human association alone (23, Corporation Street is the prime example).

My favourite Sheffield house? The Bishops' House comes top of my list, with the parlour of Carbrook Hall my favourite room. The recently published new statutory list of buildings of special architectural or historic interest by the Department of National Heritage brings a presumption in favour of the conservation of a building. We can be assured, then, that those listed here (detailed at the end of appropriate entries) are fairly safe for the foreseeable future.

I have opted for a geographical rather than chronological order. Starting in the east we travel generally anticlockwise to form a vague circuit ending not far from our starting point.

## Manor Lodge

Though now a shattered ruin Manor Lodge remains as Sheffield's second most important historic building, only slightly subordinate to the remnants of the Castle which lurk under Castle Market near the Lady's Bridge crossing of the River Don.

Built in 1516 by the fourth Earl of Shrewsbury as a pleasant alternative to the valley bottom Castle site Manor Lodge stands at over 500 feet above sea level. It takes a strong imagination these days to picture the 2,500 acres of parkland in which the mansion stood, punctuated with avenues of walnuts and magnificent oaks.

Highlights in the house's story were the detention for eighteen days in 1530 of Cardinal Wolsey, when he was on the way to London after falling foul of Henry VIII; the confinement of Mary Queen of Scots from November 1570 for most of the following fourteen years; and the start of the piecemeal demolition of the house in 1708, by then the property of the Duke of Norfolk. Various tenants altered, adjusted and quarried the site for a couple of centuries. The great gale of 1793 flattened one of the tall, brick-faced octagonal towers on the west face.

The jagged ruins we see today adjacent to the top of Manor Lane are a pathetic reminder of time's passage and the temporary nature of great wealth and power. Happily the Turret House within the grounds (built 1574, probably as a new gatehouse-cum-hunting tower) was fully restored twenty years ago and was open to the public until Sheffield City Council's parlous financial state put an end to that luxury.

*Manor Lodge is Listed Grade II and is also a Scheduled Ancient Monument.*
*Turret House is Listed Grade II★.*

## Queen's Tower

About a mile to the south west of Manor Lodge, across Norfolk Park and overlooking the heavily industrialised lower Sheaf Valley, stands a most remarkable house. It reminds us of one successful Sheffield industrialist's admiration for Mary Queen of Scots.

Samuel Roberts was born in Sheffield in 1763 and set up in silver plating as a young man; his wife was wealthy in her own right and when past seventy Roberts was able to realise his dream of commemorating his heroine, the Scottish Queen, in a a stone mansion (designed by Doncaster architects Woodhead and Hurst). It is embattled, has towers and turrets and Roberts has a fragment of old wall and a mullioned window from Manor Lodge erected in the grounds. The entire undertaking was a sensitive man's way of both honouring Mary Queen of Scots and showing his deep disapproval of the way in which Manor Lodge had been allowed to decay. The house was completed in 1837 but Roberts never occupied his Queen's Tower, instead it was a wedding present to his only son, also Samuel, who lived here until his death in 1887. His own son (who became Sir Samuel Roberts, J.P. M.P. for Ecclesall 1902-23) then came to live here. He was a barrister and director of many Sheffield companies and Lord Mayor 1899-1900. He died in 1926 and since that time the formal pastoral and wooded surroundings have been swamped by the Norfolk Park council estate, complete with overbearing tower blocks.

Queen's Tower has had various uses - warehouse, offices and, since 1978, a country club and sports centre. At the time of writing (summer 1996) plans are afoot to refurbish it for use as a leisure centre.

*Queen's Tower is Listed Grade II.*

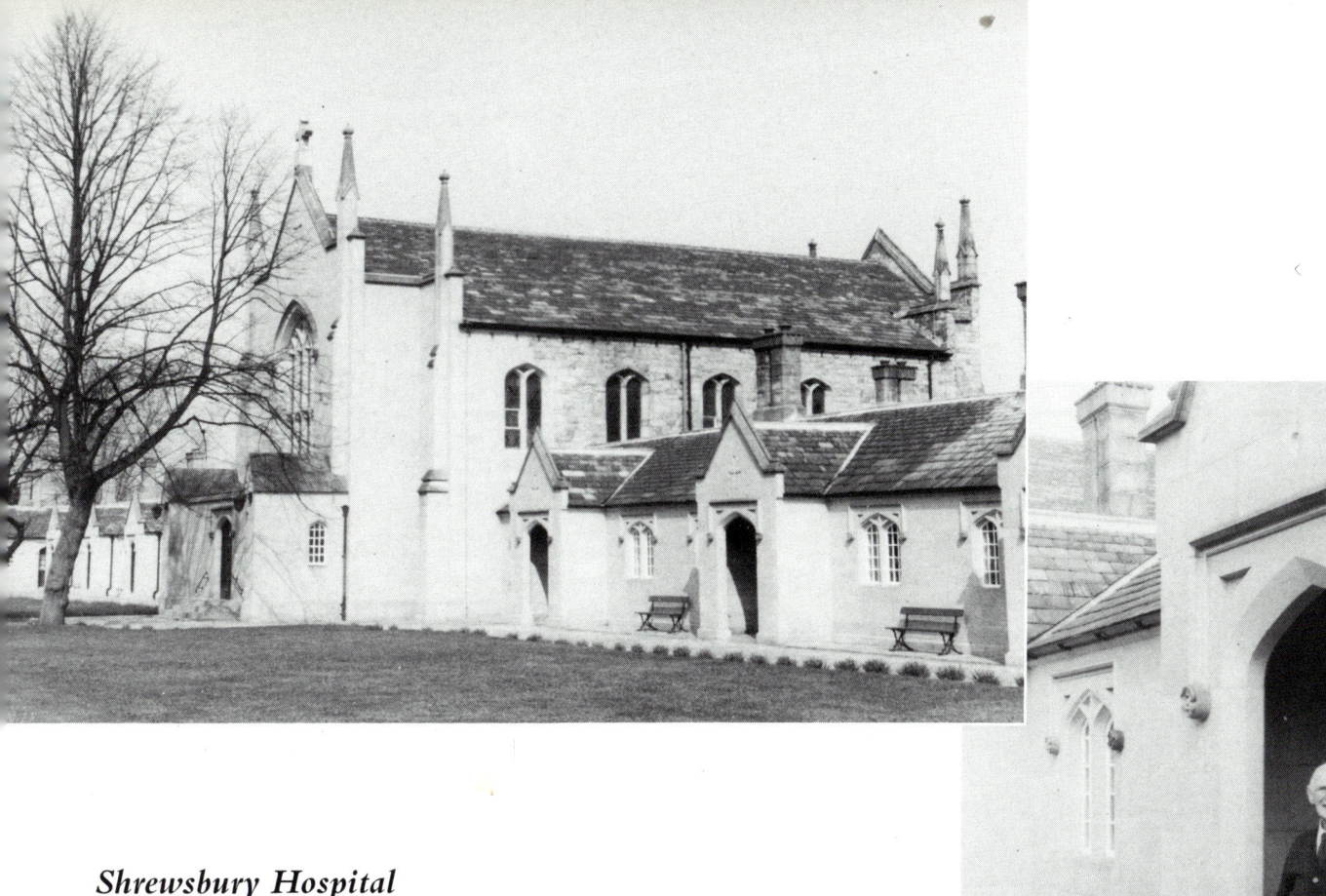

## Shrewsbury Hospital

J. D. Campbell's father and grandfather were gamekeepers at Arundel for the Duke of Norfolk. When J. D. left school in 1924 he was sent north to work in the Duke's Estate Office in Sheffield and has worked and lived in city ever since. Now he is a resident in the Shrewsbury Hospital Almshouses, Norfolk Road.

When Gilbert, seventh Earl of Shrewsbury died in 1616 he left instructions for the establishment of a hospital for twenty of Sheffield's poorest people. Insufficient funds meant his intention was deferred until 1665, when such a building was erected where the Parkway roundabout now stands, close to Sheaf Market. The site was prone to flooding so a new hospital was built beside Norfolk Road between 1823 and 1827. There is a central chapel with wings containing 36 dwellings and a Chaplain's House at one end and Infirmary at the other. When first occupied they were considered very superior, though the often infirm inmates had to climb ladders to bedrooms under the roof. Later refurbishment included the fitting of a new bathroom and bedroom behind each little house.

It was in the seventeenth century that the Shrewsbury estates came by marriage to the Duke of Norfolk and, though the Shrewsbury Hospital Trust is not part of the Duke of Norfolk's estate, the Duke is the main trustee.

*Shrewsbury Hospital is Listed Grade II.*

## Old Queen's Head

Sheffield must have been a town of timber-framed houses, slowly replaced by stone and brick ones so that now only one town centre example remains. Built about 1475 it used to be known as "The Hawle in the Pondes" and a record exists describing it as "formerly the wash-house to Sheffield Manor".

Standing adjacent to Pond Hill, not far from the Bus Station, the Old Queen's Head Hotel has an attractive timbered front range with first floor over-sailing on a coving, dressed stone gables topped by a slate roof. The house was reduced in size when the road at Pond Hill was widened in the last century.

It is remarkable that this fairly modest relic has survived at what is now a very bust spot. When first built the house must have been surrounded by riverside fields, near the track leading to Sheffield Castle and Lady's Bridge over the Don. Restoration in 1949 revealed several hidden features, including a stone fireplace that was fitted when the house was new. Being a public house it is easily possible to view part of the interior of this, the oldest house of central Sheffield.

*The Old Queen's Head Hotel is Listed Grade II★.*

## Leader House

An unlikely Georgian survivor is this lofty brick town house with raised stone quoins now looking over the whizzing traffic on Arundel Gate, its back towards Surrey Street.

Owned by the Duke of Norfolk it was built in 1770 and leased by Thomas Leader from 1777 when he moved from Essex to Sheffield to set up in business as a silversmith in this acknowledged centre of the silver trade. A decade or so later alterations enlarged the rear of Leader House and a bay window was added on the north side, now overlooking the blocked-off end of Surrey Street.

The family sold their town house in 1817 and several families lived here until it was sold to Sheffield Corporation in 1938. The demolition hammer almost fell on the building in 1970 when Sheffield Corporation sought permission to flatten what was already a listed building. This was refused and Leader House has been used by the City Polytechnic (now Hallam University) ever since. Though inauspiciously situated nowadays it is as fine an example of a Georgian town house as any in the city.

*Leader House is Listed Grade II.*

## Old Bank House

When built in 1728 this tall house stood alone in large grounds to the north of the parish church (now the Cathedral). Brick with stone quoins and ornamented with pilasters on its south front it exhibits a transitional style at the very beginning of true Georgian. It was put up for Nicholas Broadbent and his wife (who had grown rich in foreign trade) as a town house and, standing on ground which falls away behind, has deep vaulted cellars.

Here was established one of Sheffield's early private banks in 1771, by Thomas Broadbent, grandson of the builder. This Thomas must have been something of an entrepreneur because he continued to develop nearby Paradise Square at the same time (see page 11). The good times didn't last. In 1780 the Broadbent bank collapsed and its owner went into decline. Subsequently Broadbent House was occupied by various merchants and the remains of a crane still exists in the front attic, where merchandise was hoisted up and down.

Like so many old and new buildings on Hartshead this one is now offices.

*Old Bank House (Broadbent House) is Listed Grade II★.*

## The North Side of Paradise Square

Here, to the north-west of the Cathedral, between Campo Lane and Queen Street, is Sheffield's finest grouping of Georgian town houses. Other such squares exist in this country but this one has the unusual benefit of occupying a fairly steep slope. Formerly a farm field (Hick's Stile Field) the entrepreneur son of Nicholas Broadbent obtained a lease for the land in 1736 and put up the first five houses on the north side of the square. A much bigger scheme followed in 1771 when Broadbent's son, Thomas, built the houses on the remaining three sides of the square, in the same year that he opened his ill-fated bank (see page 10).

The most interesting houses in the square are those connected with famous people, as detailed on plaques on some of the buildings:
West side. No. 24. Sir Francis Chantrey (1781-1841) (see page 48) rented a room here as a studio in 1802 where he painted many local portraits for modest fees in the days before he became the country's best known sculptor.
South side. No. 3. John Wesley preached here in 1779 to 'the largest congregation he ever saw on a weekday'.
East side. No. 12. Doctor D. D. Davies (1778-1841), physician, liven here between 1803 and 1818. He translated Pinel's 'Treatise on Insanity' and assisted at the birth of the future Queen Victoria in 1819.
*All the houses in Paradise Square are Listed Grade II★.*

## The Mount

When Sheffield architect William Flockton designed and built The Mount, overlooking Glossop Road at Broomhill, it was nicknamed 'Flockton's Folly' because it was considered so far out of town as to be unattractive to buyers. Flockton was following the fashion set by Bath's Royal Crescent and London's Regent's Park. The Mount, built 1830-32, was set alone to emulate a country house, with great views over the Porter Valley. It contained eight house within a building of $2\frac{1}{2}$ storeys, 17 bays long, the central pediment supported by 6 Ionic columns. The end pavilions also have Ionic columns.

    Contrary to expectations it established Flockton as an important architect and was a sort of model for his even more ambitious Grammar School (King Edward VII School) put up soon afterwards (1838-40) a stone's throw down the road. One of the first residents was the poet and hymn writer James Montgomery who came to Sheffield from Scotland in 1792. He moved to The Mount in 1835 and died there in 1854. Other residents included Headmasters, ministers and landed gentry. My maternal great grandmother, Rachel Dearden, lived here for a time after leaving Jordanthorpe Hall, Norton.

    Eventually it was purchased by John Walsh Ltd when their High Street store (now House of Fraser) was destroyed in the Sheffield blitz in 1940. In 1958 United Steels acquired it and it eventually became the regional Headquarters of the British Steel Corporation. In 1978 it was sold again and is now insurance offices.

*The Mount is Listed Grade II★.*

## Broom Hall

Broom Hall is one of Sheffield's most important houses on account of its origins, human associations and as an example of sensitive restoration. It stands in the leafy stone suburb created in the middle of the last century on part of the estate, at the junction of Park Lane and Broomhall Road.

The earliest part of the house dates from about 1500 when it stood at the heart of a considerable estate that extended from the River Don near Sheffield Castle to Crooksmoor (north-west of the main University buildings). After ownership by the powerful de Ecclesalls it passed by marriage to the Wickersleys and then the Swyfts. Robert Swyft came to live at Broom Hall in 1532, after which he became an important resident - both a Capital Burgess of the town and Agent for the Castle. There seem to have been few sons in the succession story here so that it passed through the Jessops to the Reverend James Wilkinson in the middle of the eighteenth century.

Wilkinson was a colourful character. He was the Vicar of Sheffield between 1754 and his death in 1805. As a magistrate he was notorious for the harshness of his sentencing and in 1791 a mob descended on Broom Hall, attempting to burn it down. Some damage was done before a company of dragoons arrived and put the crowd to flight. One of the presumed ring leaders was later hanged. A major extension was added as an east wing in the late eighteenth century, during Wilkinson's ownership (the major feature above, left, and on the front cover).

During the early part of the last century Broom Hall was divided into three separate dwellings and the new owner, John Watson of Shirecliffe Hall, began granting building leases in 1829 on the surrounding farmland for the substantial houses we see today. Its history during the twentieth century has been one of decline, threat of demolition and eventual rescue and complete restoration by the internationally famous designer David Mellor who made it his home and base for cutlery manufacture. Today it is divided into offices.

The original sixteenth century block to the west has a magnificent close-studded gable overlooking the rear garden, complete with square oriel window (above right). On the south front there is an original stone gable, a projecting seventeenth century gable containing a remarkably large sundial, and the end of the large east wing added about 1790.

Broom Hall is Listed Grade II★.

## 23, Corporation Street

A terrace house on the corner of Corporation Street and Spring Street is an unlikely subject for inclusion here but No. 23, Corporation Street's claim to fame is simply because it was George Mooney's home for several years. It was a focal point in the notorious Sheffield gang wars of the twenties.

High unemployment after the Great War encouraged the so-called 'tossing rings' on Sky Edge, near Manor Lodge, and in other places. Bets were taken on the probability of which way a tossed coin would land on the ground. George Mooney (1890-1961) became the 'leader' of such a 'tossing ring'. By 1923 gambling money was short and Mooney and his associates needed a bigger share of the reduced takings; this led to conflict with the rival Park Brigade based in the Park district, close to Sky Edge.

In 1923 Mooney had moved to No. 23, Corporation Street, previously occupied as a beerhouse by his mother. Not far away other members of his gang were living. Things came to a head early on the morning of June 16th, 1923 when the Park Brigade laid siege to the house. Broken windows and ripped up gratings terrified the inmates (Mooney and his second wife) and a member of the attacking Park Brigade lay on the pavement with bullet wounds. A subsequent search of No. 23 revealed 'a miniature arsenal' of firearms and truncheons. Mooney was subsequently fined £10 for possession of firearms and five members of the Park Brigade were bound over in the sum of £20 for twelve months for 'unlawfully and tumultuously assembling outside No. 23, Corporation Street.'

For the rest of 1923 Mooney's house took on the the character of a mini-fortress with the family well and truly barricaded against the Park Brigade. Windows were broken by thrown bricks in early August and later that month a brick thrown at Mooney's wife caused head injuries. Christmas Eve saw renewed activity when Park Brigade members smashed their way into the house but they didn't find Mooney hiding in a bedroom cupboard. So they smashed the place up and fled before the police arrived. Two of the attackers were later given three months hard labour but Mooney was now a fugitive under police protection. In the New Year of 1924 Mooney disappeared from Sheffield for a year and the Park Brigade had taken over the Sky Edge 'tossing ring'.

A murder in Princess Street, off Attercliffe Road, in April, 1925 resulted in two men being hanged for the crime and marked the beginning of the end for these particular Sheffield gangs. In the spring of 1927 Mooney was imprisoned for two months for assaulting a policeman but he eventually kept out of further trouble and went to live at Rose Street, off Langsett Road.

No. 23, Corporation Street still exists but hasn't been a private house for many, many years. Anyone interested in greater detail of the gang wars should read J. P. Bean's excellent book 'The Sheffield Gang Wars' (D & D Publications, 1981).

## Carbrook Hall

Anyone travelling along Attercliffe Common might well not cast a second glance at the public house to the north side of the road called Carbrook Hall. It is, though, one of the city' historic gems which has been all but inundated by the flood of urbanisation that's transformed the lower Don Valley in the last century and a half.

In the late twelfth century the Blunts lived here at Carbrook, in the late Middle Ages a fine timber framed house was put up and in 1623 a new stone wing was added. By this time a branch of the illustrious Bright family of Whirlow lived here (see page 37). John Bright of Carbrook was a Parliamentarian in the Civil War, promoted to Colonel in 1643 and made Governor of Sheffield Castle a year later. Carbrook was used by the Parliamentarians during the siege of Sheffield Castle in 1644.

A descendent of the Brights, Admiral Southeron, sold the estate in 1819 and by 1855 the hall had become a public house and the former farm fields and grounds were being developed – this was fast becoming the heart of the world's premier steel making centre.

Don't be misled by exterior appearances, though. The parlour of Carbrook Hall is what Pevsner described as representing 'the pre-classical seventeenth century better than any other at Sheffield'. There is an excellent moulded plaster ceiling, oak panelled walls and a carved oak fireplace. Upstairs is another fine panelled room and stone chimneypiece. Though the earlier half-timbered part of the house was pulled down about 1800 this 1623 block is a grand remnant; but nowadays we have to imagine the scratching hens in the stackyard and the pastures running down to the banks of the meandering Don.

Carbrook Hall is Listed Grade II*.

## *Birley Old Hall*

High on the crest of Birley Edge at 600 feet above sea level, three miles north-west of central Sheffield, stands the old hamlet of Birley. It has a hard, stony, northern feel about it - little farms, the rather grand Birley House (now Birley Court) and Birley Old Hall.

The Old Hall is L shaped in plan, set into the crest of the ridge beside Edge Lane with its back sensibly turned to the north-west, the 'weather' direction. One wing is of oaken cruck construction, suggesting it was constructed in the late Middle Ages. On the outside of the north-western corner a portion of cruck timber is clearly visible.

J. Carr built a new, rather grander wing at right angles to the original in 1705 with upright two-light mullioned windows and subsequently the place has had a kaleidoscopic history. Eventually purchased by Sheffield Corporation it was leased to Messrs. Daniel Doncaster in 1959 as offices. A tide of council housing swept up the slope from Birley Carr and now comes right up to the Old Hall's little garden. The present owner arrived in 1982 and has totally restored the house - the original wing has the cosy feel of an ancient farmhouse, the 1705 addition has restrained elegance. In the garden is the restored gazebo called the Falconry, also built about 1705.

*Birley Old Hall and the Falconry are Listed Grade II.*

## Wadsley Hall

Not so long ago Wadsley was a little village separated from Sheffield by the tilting fields and woods that lay above the River Don. The Hall, in Far lane, originated in medieval times and was later owned by the Earls of Shrewsbury, then passing to the Dukes of Norfolk.

Two famous men were born at the Hall, which had been rebuilt in 1722 in a style similar to the 1705 wing of Birley Old Hall (see opposite) so the same architect may have been responsible for both. Thomas Creswick was born here in 1811 and made a name for himself as a landscape painter in London, becoming R. A. in 1851.

The Fowlers had been connected with Wincobank for over two centuries and John Fowler served with the Ecclesfield Volunteers during the Napoleonic wars, later becoming a land surveyor. He moved to live at Wadsley Hall on becoming married in 1815, where he enjoyed 'the comfort of a large family circle'. His eldest son, John, was born at the Hall in 1817 and he, too, enjoyed the 'sane and healthy surroundings of his home'. He left Wadsley at the age of seventeen to work as a civil engineer in many parts of the country and became Sir John Fowler, designer of the Forth Railway Bridge.

In later life he recounted an incident that took place while he was visiting his family at Wadsley Hall. The time was mid century and railway mania was at its height. It was the dead of night when the young Fowler was roused from sleep by a visitor who had arrived by coach-and-four requesting that he undertake the engineering of a new line from Leeds to Glasgow. The visitor had an order for £20,000 as a payment on account for the survey expenses. Fowler prudently declined what must have been a tempting offer and the coach-and-four drove off into the night. Huge problems with the eventual construction of this line over the Pennines proved Fowler's wisdom.

The Fowlers continued to occupy the Hall until after the Great War (during which time it housed Belgian refugees) and has since had several owners.

*Wadsley Hall is Listed Grade II.*

## Loxley House

The Rev. Thomas Halliday, one time Unitarian minister at Norton, built a house for himself in 1795. It was a fairly imposing building, at the top of a drive that swept up from Wadsley's Ben Lane. In 1808 it was sold to Thomas Payne and this family rebuilt it as Loxley House in 1826, much grander than the original with three storeys and three wide-set bays. The most striking feature is the Venetian windows on the front elevation. The high rear wing is obviously older and massively barn-like.

Uncleaned, the house retains its sooty coat and seems all the more grim for that. By 1865 the eccentric Dr. Henry Payne was living here in some style and, having fallen out with the vicar of Wadsley, was buried in his own grounds without any ceremony in 1895.

Alderman William Clegg, a solicitor, arrived in 1895 and was followed by two other parties upto the outbreak of the Great War but they seem to have been tenants because during that war two of Dr. Payne's spinster nieces lived here - the last time it was a private house. In 1919 the Cripples Aid Association took it over and later it became the headquarters for Sheffield Sea Cadets.

Though the little park surrounding the mansion remains and keeps urban development somewhat at arm's length Loxley House has the air of genteel decay, an estate that has seen better days. In winter there's melancholy under the gaunt trees that break the winds that blow down Bradfield Dale. It was put up for sale in summer, 1996.

*Loxley House is Listed Grade II.*

## *The Towers*

William C. Leng (1824-1902) arrived in Sheffield in 1864 and eventually took over the Sheffield Daily Telegraph with a partner. Being an early campaigning journalist he arrived in the city just at the right time to do much investigative work into the collapse of Dale Dike Reservoir in Bradfield Dale, in March 1864. Leng was eventually rewarded with a Knighthood.

One of his sons Christopher D. Leng (1861-1921) succeeded his father as Editor and joint owner of the Sheffield Daily Telegraph. Keen on agriculture he built The Towers in 1896, near the junction of Sandygate Road with Coldwell Lane. Leng was a romantic, the form of his new Scottish Baronial style house proclaims that! Built on a high knoll the lofty tower is still a conspicuous landmark. There was a little farm here, too, with 'model dairy' where the latest ideas in milk handling and processing were used. Leng came to be known as something of a pioneer of the dairy industry.

Around the estate perimeter a low curtain wall was erected with a small tower at each angle (originally there was eight of these). A keen golfer Leng was instrumental in founding the Hallamshire Golf Club nearby and in 1913 got involved in saving Endcliffe Hall from demolition (see pages 22 and 23).

His last enterprise was the laying out of the estate of bungalows at Den Bank, overlooking the Rivelin Valley below The Towers (1920-21). On New Year's Day, 1921 he died suddenly, aged 59. After various uses his remarkable house was opened by Sheffield Corporation as a centre for handicapped children in 1954. It has recently been sold and is being restored as a private house (summer, 1996).

*The Towers is Listed Grade II.*

## Tapton Hall

Shore Lane climbs steeply from Fulwood Road to Manchester Road and half way up, on a sunny shelf to the west, stands Tapton Hall. The original house was occupied by Dame Shore (hence Shore Lane), Florence Nightingale's grandmother. The young Florence often stayed here at Tapton. Dame Shore died in 1853, aged 96.

Edward Vickers (1804-97), true father of one of Sheffield's greatest steel dynasties, totally rebuilt Tapton Hall in 1855 and twelve year later sold it to George Wilson (1802-78, partner in the old snuff firm of Wilson of Sharrow Mills. Wilson paid £3,500 for Tapton Hall, plus £1,424 for the furniture and £218 for the wine left in the cellar.

George Wilson's son, George Kingsford Wilson (1853-1933), married Florence Dixon, a daughter of Henry Dixon of Stumperlowe Hall (see pages 30 and 31) and they occupied the house later. Incidentally, when George Kingsford Wilson died in 1933 his coffin was carried in the traditional family way by six snuff grinders, up the hill from Sharrow Mills to Ecclesall church.

George Kingsford Wilson's son was George Ronald Wilson (1888-1958), a bachelor, and he lived at Tapton all his life. Injuries received in the Great War resulted in eventual loss of both legs but he managed to carry on fly fishing and shooting; the latter from a swivel chair carried to the butts. George Ronald Wilson died suddenly at Tapton in 1958. Soon afterwards the house was purchased by the Sheffield Masonic Lodge and two large monolithic extensions were added on the east and west sides of the Victorian block in 1967.

*Tapton Hall is Listed Grade II.*

## Thornbury

Virtually adjacent to Tapton Hall, a few hundred yards to the south-west, Sir Frederick Thorpe Mappin commissioned M. E. Hadfield and Son to design a new house which was built 1864-5. He called it 'Thornbury'.

Mappin was the eldest son of Joseph Mappin of the famous firm of cutlers and silversmiths. His uncle was John Newton Mappin, best remembered as the man who bequeathed his painting collection (valued at more than £80,000) to initiate the Mappin Art Gallery, Weston Park. Sir Frederick Thorpe Mappin had been involved with the family business but later acquired the steel firm of Thomas Turton of Sheaf Works, near the Canal Basin. His was an illustrious career; Master Cutler in 1855, Mayor of Sheffield 1877-78, Director of the Midland Railway. In 1880 he was elected a Liberal MP for Bassetlaw and East Retford, five years later as Liberal MP for Hallam.

As advocate of temperance he established in 1877 his own Cocoa and Coffee House at Highfield, the first in Sheffield. At the opening of the Mappin Art Gallery in 1877 Sir Frederick added to his late uncle's gift by presenting a further 48 paintings from his own collection.

Thornbury is a big, bold, stone house with curving bays looking out over what is now a mature garden. In 1949 it was acquired as a children's hospital and since recent enlargements and restoration is a private hospital.

## Endcliffe Hall

In the middle of the nineteenth century wealthy landowners and industrialists put up numerous stone mansions, particularly in the cleaner, western suburbs. There's a concentration of these on Fulwood Road in the Ranmoor and Endcliffe districts.

Probably the most astonishing is the one built for Sir John Brown (1816-1896) by Sheffield architect Flockton and Abbott on the site of what is now called 'old Endcliffe Hall' (probably early Georgian). Brown's new Endcliffe Hall was built in two years (1863-65), complete with 160 foot long conservatory, coach house and stables. This period has been described as one of 'unparalleled grandeur' when for some years the 'palaces at Endcliffe' were the scene of splendid occasions and famous and influential world figures 'were received in elegant Italianate drawing rooms' filled with the most expensive works of art.

Endcliffe Hall is an Italianate gem with intact, airy (bleak?) rooms which still give a good insight into what the newly completed house was like. But it almost ended in oblivion. After the death of Lady Brown in 1881 Sir John lost much of his former vitality and spent increasingly long periods in the south. In 1892 he left Endcliffe Hall forever and it was put on the market by London auctioneers Maple and Company. The new house had cost Sir John Brown about £160,000, including furnishings, and Maple and Company were now seeking only £70,000.

It was offered to Sheffield City Council with the suggestions that they might use it as hospital asylum, technical college, museum and library - the possibilities seemed endless. The Council scoffed at the idea and turned down the offer.

In April, 1893 the contents of the house went in a five day sale. Most of these contents were sold at what now seem giveaway prices - 90 yards of Axminster carpet from the drawing room had cost £1.75 a square yard when new and now made a total of only £24! In July, 1895 the Hall and 33 acres were sold for £26,000 to a syndicate of local businessmen (which included Sir Robert Abbot Hatfield - see page 40) who had their eyes on the development potential of 20 acres.

By the following year Sheffield City Council had approved the development of Endcliffe Park Avenue, Endcliffe Grove Avenue and Endcliffe Hall Avenue; within four years the present residential pattern we now see in the area had been established. Meanwhile, Sir John Brown died at the end of December 1896 and was brought from Kent to be buried in Ecclesall parish churchyard (right).

As Hindmarch and Podmore have pointed out in their study of Endcliffe Hall, within thirty years (1865-95) the status of what had been 'the foremost residence in Sheffield' declined 'to that of prime land ripe for development'.

The house was used for a few years for exhibitions and dances but by 1913 it was again threatened with demolition. Christopher D. Leng of The Towers, Sandygate (see page 19), led a campaign to save the hall. The former Commanding Officer of the 4th (Hallamshire) Battalion The York and Lancaster Regiment (Territorial Force) was keen that Endcliffe Hall should replace the Hyde Park Barracks as their headquarters and in January, 1914 approval was given by the War Office. It has been owned by them ever since, now called the Yorkshire and Humberside TAVRA.

Surprisingly for such a large house it's virtually impossible to see Endcliffe Hall from any public road (there's a glimpse from Endcliffe Hall Avenue).
*Endcliffe Hall is Listed Grade II★.*

*Rachel Redfern*

## Oakbrook

Mark Firth's giant steel works was expanding alongside John Brown's in the city's Don Valley in the middle of the nineteenth century. Here was another magnate looking for the site for an impressive new mansion and he, too, chose land adjacent to Fulwood Road. He purchased 26 acres and employed Flockton and Son to design his new home.

This house, like Brown's, was Italianate with a tower and porte-cochere, and was completed in 1860 (ahead of Endcliffe Hall by a couple of years) and this must have pleased Firth. Another feather in Firth's cap came in 1875 when the Prince and Princess of Wales (later King Edward VII and Queen Alexandra) chose to stay at Oakbrook rather than at Endcliffe Hall when they visited Sheffield. But that was understandable because the main purpose of their visit was to open Firth Park.

Mark Firth suffered a stroke at his works in 1880 and lay for twelve days at Oakbrook before eventually succumbing. His widow, Caroline, lived on there for almost fourteen years but after her death in 1894 it was sold to William S. Laycock (1843-1916), grandson of the well established hair seat manufacturer Samuel Laycock. William set out to fill a niche in the market for comfort for railway passengers. He made window blinds and other carriage fittings and built the new Victoria Works, Archer Road in 1901 (demolished 1996). Laycock died in 1916 and Oakbrook was used as a hospital and convalescent home for army officers. In 1919 it became the Convent of Notre Dame, many sisters based there teaching at Notre Dame High School in the city. Each summer pupils went to Oakbrook for Sports Day (the photograph above was taken in 1927); in 1935 new buildings housed part of the High School at Oakbrook and eventually the entire school moved there and the Sisters moved away. St. Marie's Primary School is also accommodated in Oakbrook's former grounds.

*Oakbrook is Listed Grade II.*

## Riverdale House

This typically flamboyant Victorian house in Gothic Revival style was built about 1860 for Charles Henry Firth, beside Graham Road near Nether Green. The front overlooks the woods of the Porter Valley and Bingham Park. In 1902 the successful businessman John George Graves moved here, best remembered as one of the city's most generous benefactors. Among other things he presented the Norton Hall estate (now called Graves Park) in 1925 and his valuable collection of painting to the Graves Art Gallery in the city centre (opened in 1934).

His rapidly expanding business included manufacture and sales of furniture, electro-plated goods, tools, drapery and clothes, and a new printing department produced his catalogues. Altogether Graves rented 27 premises in the city, all manufacturing these goods. By the year he moved into Riverdale House he had a turnover of £1 million.

But things started to go wrong. In 1908 financial embarrassment forced him to lease Riverdale and he moved to a smaller house in Beauchief. By 1915 Graves was able to return to Riverdale where he lived for the rest of his life. After his death in 1945, aged almost 79, Riverdale became offices and the former large grounds where his staff had once enjoyed an annual tea party was filled by the Riverdale private flat complex which surrounds and comes within a few yards of the old house.
*Riverdale House is Listed Grade II.*

## Oak House

Here's an unusual house, tucked in against a mature spinney at the top of Carsick Hill Way, above Ranmoor. It has the appearance of a beautifully proportioned Elizabethan half-timbered building but was, in fact, built in 1990! Oak House does justice to its owners who weren't content to erect a boring new house like thousands of others. Instead green English oak was used in the traditional way to construct the framework, but with the benefit of modern insulation.

Standing on a sloping site it's been possible to use split-level design, so adding greater character. An altogether successful modern dwelling that others would do well to emulate in the future.

## Stumperlowe Cottage

The late Bessie Bunker came across Stumperlowe Cottage when she was gathering information in the late sixties for her book on the cruck buildings of the district. She found a cottage and attached barn behind the present Stumperlowe Hall, in Fulwood, and there were four sets of curving oaken cruck timbers remaining (below).

Mrs Bunker considered this the original 'hall' and after the newer Stumperlowe Hall was built about 1650 it became a labourer's cottage and attached barn. She considered it was from about that time that the ancient cruck building (probably dating from about 1400) started to deteriorate. The ancient trackway linking Hallam Head with High Storrs, Ecclesall passed in front of Stumperlowe Cottage but Victorian and later building has obliterated this, and the extensive lands of this historic farm.

By the time of Mrs Bunker's visit Stumperlowe Cottage was in a sorry state and much of the barn had become roofless; the ancient cruck timbers were open to the heavens. The last occupant left in 1968. Demolition seemed imminent (right).

But the story has a happy ending. Mr and Mrs D. Millar were living

next door and were able to purchase Stumperlowe Cottage. Careful and sympathetic restoration took place between 1986 and 1993; the Millars moved in at Christmas, 1993 (opposite). Entering the restored house you get a shock because the entire former barn is an open living space with three of the remaining sets of cruck timbers soaring to the roof, creating the sense of an old-timed vaulted hall. Standing with your back to the fireplace at the western end the roof ridge timbers make a six feet curve from one end to the other.

Further west the rooms in the former cottage section conform to those in the original, looking out through small windows onto the intimate walled garden.

*Stumperlowe Cottage is Listed Grade II.*

## *Stumperlowe Hall*

Though the Mitchells owned property here at Stumperlowe, Fulwood as early as 1397 the house we see today, looking up the drive from the gateway at the junction of Slayleigh Lane with Stumperlowe Hall Road, was put up as late as 1650 by Robert Hall, a descendent of the Mitchells. By 1716 these Halls had to surrender Stumperlowe by order of the Sheffield Manor Court and for most of that century it was the home of lead merchant called John Hawksworth.

    The great metamorphosis took place when Henry Isaac Dixon of Page Hall, Pitsmoor bought and rebuilt the house in 1854. It is fortunate that he used a fairly restrained and sympathetic style though the enlarged fenestration cannot be as attractive as the original mullioned windows. Dixon did a lot for Fulwood - tree planting and a generous benefactor of Christ Church - before his death in 1912. After his son left the house in 1924 it was home to several families in turn before Sir George and Lady Kenning arrived in 1957. Lady Kenning died in 1974 and Cams have done much since their arrival to keep the house and grounds in fine condition.

*Stumperlowe Hall is Listed Grade II.*

## Fulwood Hall

High up on the breezy, northern slope of the Mayfield Valley this grand old house, not unlike the original Whirlow Hall (see page 37), existed in the late fifteenth century but seems to have been much altered in 1620. Certainly the exterior suggests an early seventeenth century date.

The Fox family lived here until 1707, when the spendthrift George Fox had to sell up. After this Fulwood was home to many families, purchased in 1942 by Morgan Fairest. It is architecturally typical of many large yeoman farmer's houses in this part of the country, with nicely proportioned mullioned windows with diamond shaped leaded lights.

The house looks out over a modest, sloping garden to the tilting, stone walled pastures of this Peak District borderland. It is still easy to imagine this as the home of a working farming family.

*Fulwood Hall is Listed Grade II.*

## Whiteley Wood Hall

Though Whiteley Wood Hall is no more I include it here (the only demolished house in this book) because it has so many important historical associations, and because the stable block and associated cottages remain.

It was built on the southern crest of the wooded Mayfield Valley in 1662 on land owned by Thomas Dale, on the site of an older hall-house. One of Dale's daughters married Alexander Ashton of Stoney Middleton in 1659 and they built the Hall. In 1741 the Aston's grandson conveyed the estate to Strelley Pegge but he already had his own house at Beauchief (see page 35) so sold Whiteley Wood to Thomas Boulsover, father of Sheffield Plate, in 1757. The servants were housed in nearby cottages (now called Whiteley Wood Manor and Cottages) and Boulsover remained here until his death on 9th September, 1788 aged 84.

On the death of Boulsover's great grandson in 1861 the property reverted to a distant relative. From 1864 to 1876 it was home to Samuel Plimsoll (famous as M. P. for Derby and 'the sailor's friend' who was instrumental in passing the Merchant Shipping Act and the creation of the 'Plimsoll Line' on ships).

The dreadfully hot, dry summer of 1868 prevented the South Yorkshire Miners' Association holding their Annual procession in Norfolk Park so Plimsoll invited them to process from Sheffield to Whiteley Wood Hall with twenty silk banners. By 2.0 p.m. 10,000 miners sat on the lawns in front of the house to hear rallying speeches. 'My grounds', Plimsoll later recounted, 'never look so beautiful as when occupied by Sunday School children or by such gatherings as I now saw before me.'

In 1893 the Hall became the home of my great uncle, Arnold Muir Wilson (1857-1909) and his family. He was a well known Sheffield solicitor, J. P., City Councillor, traveller and mountaineer. In 1896 the Hall was purchased by Sheffield City Council but the Wilsons continued to live there. After my great uncle's death in 1909 my great aunt restored (and presumably moved to) adjacent Whiteley Wood Manor.

In 1930 the Hall was purchased for use by Sheffield Girl Guides but due to lack of funds it steadily fell into disrepair. In 1957 the Council for the Conservation of Sheffield's Antiquities made an abortive bid to preserve the wonderful south front, considered 'an unusually sophisticated feature for a house of this type in the North of England ... and well in advance of other houses of the period in this area - for example, the Peacock Inn, Rowsley and Eyam Hall.'

The Hall was, in fact, a complex of different buildings periods and styles and photographs taken at the turn of the century show much of its exterior covered with Virginia Creeper. The photograph (above) shows my great aunt Eva Holland and her son Frank Sydney Holland about 1905 and I believe it was taken in the garden of Whiteley Wood Hall when they were visiting Eva's sister, Arnold Muir Wilson's wife. It evokes a summer afternoon in a world that totally disappeared with the outbreak of the Great War. Captain Frank Sydney Holland was killed in France on 27th November, 1917 aged 22.

Attempts to save the house failed and it was pulled down in 1957 though the Girl Guides Association still use the stables and part of the grounds.

*The late eighteenth/early nineteenth century Whiteley Wood Hall stable block is Listed Grade II.*

## Dore Moor House

Claimed as 'the most expensive property ever to go on the market in Sheffield' when it was offered for sale in 1983, this huge house has been home to several nationally important industrialists. Built in 1906 at 900 feet above sea level near the city's south-western corner, above Dore village, it was designed by Sir Edwin Lutyens's former assistant A. F. Royds. The Lutyens influence is obvious in the Old Dutch architecture but external appearance was master over internal convenience! There were seventeen bedrooms, a sitting room 68 feet long, but only one bathroom and electric light provided by an engine.

Dore Moor House was built for William James Armitage, a Director, of Brown Bayley's steel works. Soon afterwards it was sold to Daniel Doncaster and in 1920 Percy and Mrs Fawcett moved here from Whirlow Brook House (which they had built in 1906 - the same year that Door Moor House was put up, see page 36). Percy Fawcett was a Director of John Brown & Co. Ltd. and the Fawcetts stayed here until 1938, when it was purchased by Messrs. Firth Brown as their Managing Director's residence and thereafter occupied by Sir Alan J. Grant (Master Cutler, 1943), his wife and daughters. The Grants opened the 19 acres of gardens and woodland during the summer in the war years in aid of Sheffield Newspapers' War Fund.

In 1945 it became the home of Sir Eric Mensforth, Vice-Chairman of Westland Aircraft Ltd (1943-53), a Director (later Deputy Chairman) of John Brown a Co. Ltd. (1948-83) and Master Cutler (1965-66). He made changes at Dore Moor House, including the lowering of some window bases so they could be seen out of more comfortably, division of the house into his residence and the accommodation for company guests, and, in keeping with the mood of the early post-war years, he turned much of the grounds into productive farmland.

Sir Eric was at the forefront of pioneering work on helicopters at this time and on September, 18th, 1950 test pilot Alan Bristow made demonstration and passenger flights with a Westland Sikorsky from the lawn of Dore Moor House - probably the first of such flights in this country.

In 1953 Sir Charles Sykes (Managing Director of Firth Brown) and his wife moved in and reversed the residence/guest house layout. When they left for a more modest house in Dore the next Managing Director of Firth Brown, Philip Ling, took up residence and eventually, in a bid to raise capital, his company finally sold it to Broadland Properties of Scarborough in January, 1984 for £290,000. Coincidentally, it's interesting to note that none of the residents of Dore Moor House ever had a son, only daughters.

The estate was subsequently split into ten lots - the house itself divided into three substantial properties - and put up for auction in June, 1984 but only five lots were sold. The remainder were offered for sale privately and eventually everything went. Today this outstanding early twentieth century house has much the same external appearance as ninety years ago, but is a sort of residential complex, home to half a dozen families.

## Beauchief Hall

Twelfth century Beauchief Abbey was quarried to provide building stone when Edward Pegge erected Beauchief Hall nearby in 1671.

Though the estate here was owned by the Strelleys from 1573 it passed through marriage 75 years later to the Pegges and, with a slight change of name to Pegge-Burnell, they remained here until 1909 when William Wilson III, of the Sharrow Mills snuff manufacturing family, made it his family home.

William Wilson III maintained hounds at Horsleygate, Homesfield and owned Stanage and Hallam grouse moors. After his tragic death in 1927 his eldest daughter, Winifred, moved in the early thirties to Highlightley, Barlow. A gifted artist she studied under Sit John Arnesby Brown and had a large wooden studio in the garden at Beauchief. She took this to Highlightley and her cousin A. Kingsford Wilson moved to Beauchief Hall. After his death in the early fifties the house was used for a variety of purposes, including De La Salle College, a hotel and corporate headquarters.

The house was altered in 1836, including the addition of a front porch with lotus columns. The upper windows, too, were enlarged at this time. The interior contains some of the finest period rooms in the Sheffield area, including what Pevsner calls 'a sumptuous fireplace' in the former entrance hall.

Happily some of Winifred Wilson's delightful oil paintings of the house's exterior still exist; some of them showing the south front as the Virginia Creeper exploded in a riot of autumn colour.

*Beauchief Hall is Listed Grade II★.*

## Whirlow Brook House

The Whirlow district of western Sheffield has, maybe, a greater concentration of remarkable houses than any other, Here are descriptions of five of them.

Whirlow Brook House was built in 1906 by Percy Fawcett and his wife so they could move from Middlewood Hall to be near Percy's brother, who had inherited Whirlow Court (see page 39). The house and its grounds occupy what had been part of the Standhills estate, Long Line. The house is stone with long windows, set on an elevated terrace which look across the sloping grounds towards Ecclesall Woods and Abbeydale. The Fawcetts lived in their new home for fourteen years before moving to Dore Moor House. (see page 34). They were followed here by Percy Fawcett's sister, Madge, and her husband Walter Benton Jones.

The Jones's were keen gardeners and six staff were employed by Mrs Benton Jones managed and developed the grounds herself. The wonderful gardens at Whirlow Brook had reached a peak of perfection when Mrs Benton Jones died in 1938 and her husband later sold the property (which included almost 40 acres) to a consortium of the Town Trustees, the Graves Charitable Trust and Sheffield Corporation. The sale price was £15,000. The grounds were finally opened to the public as Whirlow Brook Gardens in 1951 and they remain so today; the house contains a cafe and entertaining rooms for private parties. Together they provide one of the city's finest public amenities.

## Whirlow Hall

The Bright family owned much land and property in the Sheffield area in earlier times. They are associated with Carbrook Hall (see page 15) and Banner Cross Hall (see pages 42 and 43) and here, at Whirlow Hall high on its breezy hillside site at the end of Broad Elms Lane. This was once the original through route (Fenney Lane/Broad Elms Lane) between Sheffield and the Peak District.

By the early fifteenth century the Brights were living here at Whirlow; they may have settled here a good bit earlier. They were yeoman farmers and, like some others in the district, became blacksmiths making arms as well as agricultural implements. By 1720 Henry Bright was bankrupt and his Whirlow estate was sold to Sir John Statham. The Hall here at the time had been erected in Elizabethan times with large rooms - Shirley Frost has pointed out in her fine history of Whirlow that one of the rooms was 27 feet wide and had a window with 470 panes!

Sir John Statham didn't hold onto the estate very long, selling it on to Thomas Hollis in 1725. It passed to the Hollis Trust and the Hall was divided into apartments; it was from this time that it began to deteriorate. The east wing was demolished in 1795, the rest pulled down later. In 1843 a new, more modest house was built - the one we see now. A very attractive, well proportioned stone farmhouse whose design originates in Jacobean times.

The tenant at this time was William Furness, who was succeeded in 1895 by his son, Richard. When Richard died in 1928 he was succeeded, in turn by his son, John, who gave up the tenancy in 1937 after a family occupation of 200 years.

In 1943 Sheffield City Council bought the farm and, in 1949, the Hall itself. Since 1979 the Whirlow Hall Trust has leased it as a working farm where school parties come to experience country life and farm work at first hand.

In the yard below the Hall are Whirlow Hall Cottage (sometimes called Low House) and two ancient cruck barns. Everything is in good order, the future of this ancient site and its buildings seems secure. The photograph (above) shows the new Whirlow Hall (left) and Whirlow Hall Cottage (right) from the lower yard on an April morning.

*Whirlow Hall Cottage and outbuildings are Listed Grade II.*

## Whirlow House

Anyone travelling along Ecclesall Road South from Whirlow Bridge towards Sheffield will notice, beyond Whirlow Grange Diocesan Centre, new stone gateposts, wrought iron gates and screen walls to the left hand. Up the long drive, beyond the stand of mature trees, we glimpse the bright brick facade of a large building - a new hotel? Corporate headquarters? Not at all - this is the new Whirlow House.

The solicitor Frederick Wilson built Whirlow House here in 1841, set in more than fourteen acres. The mansion was subsequently owned by various wealthy Sheffield families and in 1902 Edgar Allen (1838-1925) made it his home. He founded his own Imperial Steel Works in 1867 and later put his success to the general good. He established the Edgar Allen Library at Sheffield's new University in 1909 and is perhaps better remembered for his Edgar Allen Institute for Medico-Mechanical Treatment opened in 1911 to provide free medical treatment in the city.

When Edgar Allen died in 1915 Whirlow House was sold to Edward Dixon of nearby Whirlow Croft and eventually purchased in 1938 by Sheffield City Council. It was used for many years by various Government Ministries and demolished in a neglected state in 1977.

In 1993 the new Whirlow House (above) was built on virtually the same site as the original by a Sheffield businessman, complete with leisure facilities of which neither Frederick Wilson or Edgar Allen would have dreamed.

## Whirlow Court

James Fawcett and his wife had the imposing stone mansion called Whirlow Court built on the south side of Ecclesall Road South in the early 1880's. The Fawcetts were joint owners of the well known cutlers and silversmiths James Dixon & Sons Ltd.

The new house had a substantial garden and parkland beyond (now much reduced by properties on Whirlow Court Road and other residential development). The Fawcetts employed a dozen staff. After James Fawcett's death in 1900 he was succeeded by his son Alfred, a solicitor, who had married the daughter of Major William Greaves Blake of Mylnhurst (see page 41). The Fawcetts finally sold Whirlow Court in 1915 and it changed hands again in 1920 when Arthur Davy, well known Sheffield grocer, moved there. After his death in 1946 it was sold to Lt. Colonel Maurice Batchelor, Chairman of Batchelor Peas.

Eventually, in 1954, Sheffield City Council purchased the house as the Lord Mayor's official residence. Nowadays it is used as the official Judges' Lodgings when visiting justices sit at Sheffield Crown Court. The house and gardens continue to be kept in excellent condition.

*Whirlow Court is Listed Grade II.*

## *Parkhead Hall*

When an architect builds a house for his own use the result can be something rather special. Such was the case when the outstanding Sheffield architect John Mitchell Withers had 'The Woodlands' built as his home in 1864-65, standing with its back to Ecclesall Road South near what is now the Parkhead traffic lights at the top of Abbey Lane. Only 28 years old when he moved in he spent the rest of his busy life there.

It is a neo-gothic fantasy, with carved human heads looking out, gargoyle like, from the eaves and the front door on the east front giving access to a lofty entrance hall. Withers was able to obtain sixteenth century oak panelling from Manor Lodge (see page 5) to furnish his dining room. The bleached exterior stone walls harmonize well with the pink roof titles.

In 1898 the property was sold to Robert Abbot Hadfield who became the world's foremost metallurgist and pioneer of alloy steels. A year later he became Master Cutler and in 1908 was knighted. Hadfield added a two storey extension and renamed the place 'Parkhead House', staying here until 1939 (a year before his death) when it fetched £6,750. It was bought as potential Judges' Lodgings but the outbreak of war prevented this and eventually, in 1948, it was adapted to a council home for elderly men. Forty years later it became vacant and was very dilapidated when purchased for £1.2 million to become the headquarters of Facia, the retail empire headed by Sheffield businessman Stephen Hinchcliffe. By the time of Facia's collapse (summer, 1996) the house was in magnificent condition, set in perfectly presented gardens and re-named Parkhead Hall.
*Parkhead Hall is Listed Grade II.*

## Mylnhurst

When Major William Greaves Blake, a veteran of the Indian Mutiny of 1857, chose the place to build his new mansion the area around Button Hill, Ecclesall was open farmland broken by pockets of woodland. Henry Vickers' house, Holmwood, had been built in 1857 some distance to the west but there was nothing between.

The year was 1883 and the new stone house was neo Gothic with a castellated tower, and called Mylnhurst. There is much ornate stonework detail (see carved pillars supporting an oriel window on the south front, left.) It was large and cost £14,000 – the Greaves Blakes needed the space as they had twelve children. After Major Greaves Blake died in 1904 his wife lived on at Mylnhurst until her death in 1920. The house was sold to W. J. Walsh, owner of the department store John Walsh, High Street, Sheffield (now House of Fraser). When the Walsh family moved to a house at Ranmoor in 1933 they sold Mylnhurst to the Sisters of Mercy for their own Convent School and Nursery, which it remains to this day.

*Mylnhurst is Listed Grade II.*

## Shirle Hill

Shirle Hill stands beside Cherry Tree Road, not far from Psalter Lane in Sharrow. Originally a modest house built in 1809 (far right in this view) it became John Brown's home as he became successful in his expanding steel manufactory in Sheffield's East End. While living here he was twice Mayor of Sheffield, entertained Lord Palmerston to discuss arms manufacture and, in 1865 (the year he left this house), was elected Master Cutler. Writing in 1969 Mary Walton explains that Sir John Brown 'left the the comfortable gentility of Shirle Hill at Sharrow for the magnificent empty spaces of Endcliffe Hall' (see pages 22 and 23). Brown's managing director, William Bragge, then moved into Shirle Hill and immediately extended the house (adding the large left wing in this view) and refronted the original part.

For many years this unusual house has been a hospital of the Area Health Authority.

## Banner Cross Hall (opposite)

Travelling the highway past Ecclesall parish church one's attention is taken by turrets punctuated by tall trees behind a high stone wall. This is Banner Cross Hall, site of the Elizabethan mansion of the powerful Brights (see page 15 and 37).

The name of the place comes from the ancient cross which stood in the grounds near the house. With the extinction of the Brights in 1748 it passed by marriage to the Scottish Murray family who landscaped the grounds and when Lt. General William Murray inherited it he employed the famous architect Sir Jeffry Wyatville to completely remodel the house in 1820. The result is a clever grouping of gables and turrets to give the illusion of a stone house much larger than is actually the case. The names of some roads reflect the Murray ownership of the land - Tullibardine Road, Dunkeld Road, etc.

Later Banner Cross Hall came to the Greaves Bagshawes of Ford Hall (Chapel en le Frith) and in 1900 it was being tenanted by Douglas Vickers J.P., son of Col. Tom Vickers, Chairman of Vickers, Sons and Maxim (see page 20).

It has been the headquarters of Henry Boot and Sons plc, builders and developers, for many years.

*Banner Cross Hall is Listed Grade II, as is the ice house in the grounds to the south-east of the house.*

## 6, Kenwood Road

Maybe not a particularly remarkable looking house No. 6, Kenwood Road is one of many built on George Wostenholm's Sharrow development mentioned below. It looks like so many erected in this district at that time; a solid, stone dwelling with generously proportioned sash windows overlooking a fairly modest garden - small gardens meant more houses per acre for the developer!

But No. 6's claim to fame is as the last home of Dr. Henry Coward, one of Sheffield's great musical names. Though he served a long apprenticeship at George Wostenholm's cutlery works and was later Headmaster of Tinsley School he turned to music, gaining his Doctorate in 1894. He's best remembered as conductor of the Sheffield Musical Union and the Sheffield Chorus, conducting the once famous 'Whitsuntide Sing' in Norfolk Park.

He moved to No. 6, Kenwood Road in 1931 and died there in June, 1944 aged 95.

## Kenwood (opposite)

As George Wostenholm's cutlery business thrived - he built his new Washington Works in Wellington Street in 1837 to supply the growing trade with the American states - he started to buy land beside Cherry Tree Lane near Sharrow Head. He laid out 'sweeping, tree-lined streets which form the nicer part of Sharrow' in preparation for speculative residential development.

By 1849 Flockton and Son had built his new house, 'Kenwood', alongside Kenwood Road, using limestone from Stanton Quarries. He employed Robert Marnock to lay out his grounds, knowing that this man had successfully planned the new Botanical Gardens. During the 1850's George Wostenholm bought up a large area between Sharrow Head, Brincliffe Edge and Abbeydale Road and it was soon developed as a middle class residential area with strict rules governing 'ungentlemanly activities' by the residents.

Wostenholm died in 1876, his third wife soon remarried and a new wing was added in 1882-3. She died in 1886 and her spinster sister, Annie Moncrieffe Rundle, inherited 'Kenwood'. She lived on here until 1922. A couple of year later the property was bought by Sheffield Refreshment Houses, serving as a temperance hotel for many years. It continues today, much enlarged, as one of the city's best hotels, enjoying the legacy of Robert Marnock's delightful grounds.

## Mount Pleasant

When Francis Hurt Sitwell built his imposing red brick house about 1770, near the bottom of Sharrow Lane, the area of Highfield was quite rural. The mansion stood on the crest of a gentle slope overlooking the meandering River Sheaf, surrounded by farmland. The town centre was visible a mile to the north.

Sitwell had been adopted by his uncle, William Sitwell of Renishaw, a trustee of the Bedlam Lunatic Asylum. The pair enjoyed a pleasant lifestyle, travelling between town houses in London, Bath and Sheffield to take part in a virtual plethora of social and cultural activities. When William Sitwell died his fortunate nephew inherited half a million pounds. John Platts of Rotherham was employed as architect for Mount Pleasant, a veritable soaring pile.

For some unexplained reason the Sitwells had sold the property by 1794 and it was thereafter owned by various families until becoming the Girls' Charity School in 1874, when it moved from its original building in St. James' Row, near the Cathedral. The Charity School became the Mount Pleasant School for Girls in 1927. After the Second World War the house was used by a succession of Government departments before degenerating into a near ruin.

Happily it was saved, restored and turned into an Adult Education and Community Centre and today rears up through three storeys from a plain sweep of surrounding sward – just as proudly as when Francis Hurt Sitwell first gazed in admiration at his new Sheffield house in 1770. *Mount Pleasant is Listed Grade II★.*

## Bishops' House

It's easy to forget that Sheffield was once a town with many half-timbered buildings, erected long before bricks came into general use. Apart from the Old Queen's Head hotel, Pond Hill (see page 8) and part of Broom Hall (see page 13) the only other survivor is the Bishops' House, Norton Lees Lane. The fact that it has survived as the city's finest half-timbered building is really a matter of chance.

Built about 1500 it was owned by the powerful Blythe family – they are remembered in the Blythe Chapel in Norton parish church – though it might not have been grand enough for the family to have occupied themselves. The house's name commemorates the fact that two of the sons of William Blythe became bishops, one of Salisbury (in 1494), one of Coventry and Lichfield (in 1503).

In 1886 the property came into the ownership of Sheffield Corporation. The large barns to the west, described by Mrs Sterndale in 1824, were afterwards demolished. For a long time it housed employees of the Recreation Department and so was largely overlooked.

In 1976 Bishops' House was completely restored and opened as one of the most attractive small museums in the country, right at the top of Meersbrook Park with its wonderful northward views over the city.

*Bishop's House is Listed Grade II★.*

## The Oakes in Norton

The Norton district, formally in Derbyshire but taken into the city in 1934, was well known for its ancient oak trees in earlier times. Originally built about 1670 The Oakes in Norton was the home of the Bagshawes for almost three centuries.

    The finely proportioned stone mansion looked out over its quiet parkland from an open sunny site. It was first remodelled in the early eighteenth century for Richard Bagshawe and again, in 1811-27, by Joseph Badger of Lancaster for Sir William and William John Bagshawe. Sir William was responsible for collecting most of the best furniture and paintings that visitors marvelled at when the house was open for inspection upto recent times.

    Sir Francis Chantrey, best known son of Norton, designed the terrace on the south front of the house. As I have written before, the estate was struck a mortal blow with the building of the by-pass in front of the house. It soon drove the Bagshawes to their quieter home at Wormhill.

    The house is now divided into several apartments, as are the several outbuildings. The once grand park lies neglected, its future uncertain. The Oaks shares the honour with Beauchief Hall (see page 35) of the loveliest noble house on the city's southern fringe; each lies at the heart of a once united estate, now all broken up. Both create reverie in the heart of a sensitive onlooker but The Oakes is the more melancholy now.

The Oakes is Listed Grade II*.